CHANGING ECOSYSTEMS

BARRIE PUBLIC LIBRARY
Enriching our Community

THIS BOOK PURCHASE WAS MADE
POSSIBLE THROUGH THE GENEROUS
SUPPORT OF

Friends of the Environment Foundation

MICHAEL BRIGHT

Heinemann Library
Chicago, Illinois

Customer service 888-454-2279
Visit our website at www.heinemannraintree.com

Edited by Pollyanna Poulter
Designed by Steven Mead and Q2A Creative Solutions
Illustrated by Stuart Jackson-Carter/The Art Agency, and Nives Porcellato and Andy Craig
Picture research by Elizabeth Alexander
Production by Alison Parsons
Originated by Dot Gradations
Printed in China by Leo Paper Group

13 12 11 10 09
10 9 8 7 6 5 4 3 2 1

Library of Congress Cataloging-in-Publication Data
Bright, Michael.
 Changing ecosystems / Michael Bright.
    p. cm. -- (Timeline. Life on earth)
 Includes bibliographical references and index.
 ISBN 978-1-4329-1652-7 (hc) -- ISBN 978-1-4329-1658-9 (pb)
 1. Ecology--Juvenile literature. I. Title.
 QH541.B735 2008
 577.2--dc22
                            2008019418

Acknowledgments
The Publishers would like to thank the following for permission to reproduce photographs: © Alamy: pp. 27 (Ron Niebrugge), 31 (Visual&Written SL), 38 (Jacques Jangoux), 43 (Shenval), 45 (Tim Cuff); © Corbis: pp. 6 (Craig Tuttle), 7 (Keren Su), 10 (Denis Scott), 21 (Jonathan Blair), 33 (Scott T. Smith), 40 and 41 (Natural Selection Robert Cable/ Design Pics), 42 (Sally A. Morgan; Ecoscene); © Dorling Kindersley: p. 20 (Jon Hughes/Bedrock Studios); © Getty Images: pp. 34 (Jewel Samad/AFP), 47 (William F. Campbell/Time Life Pictures); © Imagequestmarine.com: pp. 12 and 13 (Peter Batson); © Istockphoto: **panel backgrounds** (Kristian Sekulic), pp. 4, 14, 26, 32, and 44 **chapter openers**, and **panel backgrounds** (Tammy Peluso), 5, 9 (Petr Mašek), 17 (Chuck Spidell); © NASA: p. 15; © Naturepl.com: p. 30 (Pete Oxford); © NCSU Center for Applied Aquatic Ecology: p. 37; © Science Photo Library: pp. 11 (M.I. Walker), 16 (Chris Butler), 18 (Georgette Douwma), 22 (Christian Darkin), 36 (Bill Bachman); © The Bridgeman Art Library: p. 28 (Yale Center for British Art, Paul Mellon Collection, USA).

Cover photograph of forest fire in Yellowstone National Park, USA, reproduced with permission of © naturepl.com (Steven Fuller), and Earth from space © NASA.

The Publishers would like to thank Prof. Norman MacLeod for his invaluable help in the preparation of this book.

Every effort has been made to contact copyright holders of material reproduced in this book. Any omissions will be rectified in subsequent printings if notice is given to the Publishers.

CONTENTS

Some words are printed in bold, **like this**. You can find out what they mean in the glossary.

ECOSYSTEMS

An **ecosystem** is a geographical area where plants, animals, micro-organisms, landscape, and climate all interact. An ecosystem can be as small as a puddle or as big as a tropical rain forest. The entire surface of the Earth can be thought of as a patchwork of interconnecting ecosystems.

Ecosystems are dynamic. This means they are constantly changing. Some changes are bigger and have a greater impact than others. The changes can either boost a species' ability to survive or make it more difficult for it to live. The more specialized a species is, the less well **adapted** it is to change. In a worst-case scenario, a species could fail altogether and become extinct.

Big and small systems

Within each ecosystem are distinct **habitats**, which also vary in size. A habitat provides everything a **population** of organisms needs to live, such as oxygen or carbon dioxide, warmth, food, and shelter. The population itself is a group of organisms of the same species living in the same place at the same time. Individuals within the population can be slightly different, and they are not equal in their ability to survive and reproduce. Populations of several species living together make up a **community**. When the community interacts with the physical aspects of the habitat, such as rocks and climate, it is said to be an ecosystem.

1864
Norwegian scientists haul up a sea lily from the deep sea, previously known only as a 120 million-year-old fossil.

1977
Scientists discover deep-sea hydrothermal vent communities on the seabed near Galapagos Islands.

1979
Mineral chimneys known as "black smokers" discovered on the seabed in the Gulf of California.

1850   1950   1975   1980

Carefully balanced ecosystem

A tropical coral reef is a delicately balanced ecosystem, found only in warm, shallow seas where there are few nutrients in the water. Stony corals build the underwater landscape. Their skeletons are made of calcium carbonate. The living coral itself consists of sea anemone-like **polyps**. They have green algae living in their tissues that provide food for the polyps. The polyps also use their crown of tentacles to catch tiny organisms floating in the water.

Living on the reef are schools of brightly colored reef fishes, schools of sinister reef sharks, and armies of shrimp, crabs, and lobsters. It is such a productive system that 4,000 or more species of fish might live on a coral reef. Clown fish make their home among the tentacles of sea anemones. Moray eels slide into crevices and nurse sharks hide under overhanging corals. But all this exists on a razor's edge. A relatively small rise in the sea temperature or a change in the amount of nutrients in the water can upset the ecosystem and kill the reef.

A forest fire can change an ecosystem suddenly and dramatically. Only those organisms best adapted to the changing conditions can survive.

1984
Cold seep animal communities discovered on the floor of the Gulf of Mexico.

1990
Haakon Mosby mud volcano, with its own community of deep-sea animals, discovered on the floor of the Barents Sea.

1996
Ice worms found living on ice-like methane hydrate oozing from the sea floor in the Gulf of Mexico.

1997
Polar scientists discover Lake Vostok, a vast underwater lake containing freshwater organisms, beneath the Antarctic ice sheet.

| 1985 | 1990 | 1995 | 2000 |

Layered Earth

Earth can be divided into layers or spheres. Underlying everything at ground level is the **lithosphere**—the rocks, minerals, and soils that form the surface of the Earth. The oceans, seas, lakes, rivers, and streams make up the **hydrosphere**. The layer of gases that surrounds Earth is the **atmosphere** (gaseous envelope). Where life occurs is the **biosphere**. All of these spheres interact.

Biomes

A regional community of plants and animals with similar life forms and environmental conditions is known as a **biome**. Earth's biomes are named after the dominant life form that exists there. This is often a plant, such as grass, or a plant-like animal, such as coral.

A particular biome can be seen as similar habitats in several parts of the world. For example, **temperate** grasslands are known as the veldt in South Africa, the pampas of Argentina, the steppes of Russia, and the prairies of North America. The organisms living in a grassland habitat in one part of the world may resemble organisms living in a similar habitat in another part of the world, but they are not necessarily related. This is because they respond to similar **selection pressures** and therefore show the same **anatomical** or behavioral features.

Earth's major biomes are **tundra**, forests, grasslands, deserts, marine, and freshwater, and these can be subdivided depending on the prevalent conditions, for example, tropical or temperate, hot or cold, wet or dry.

These bottlenose dolphins breathe air yet live in the sea. It means their lives are influenced by conditions in at least two of Earth's spheres—hydrosphere and atmosphere. They are also part of the biosphere.

The Bactrian camel lives in the cold deserts of Central Asia, one of Earth's major biomes.

Biodiversity

Many different organisms populate ecosystems in each of Earth's biomes. Together they make up the planet's biodiversity. Currently, there are believed to be as many as 100 million living species on Earth, of which only 1.4 million have been discovered by science. It is this great diversity of living things that ensures life continues after any major change. If biodiversity in an ecosystem drops below a certain threshold, then the ecosystem is unable to sustain itself and species living there die out or are replaced. Because Earth is currently experiencing rapid environmental change, understanding what is happening to biodiversity across the planet is crucial and is at the center of ecological research.

GAIA HYPOTHESIS

Independent British scientist James Lovelock (born 1919) was working with NASA on methods of detecting life on Mars when he realized that the living and non-living parts of Earth can be viewed as a single interacting system. In other words, Earth is like a living organism. The Gaia **hypothesis** suggests that living things control everything on the Earth's surface, from global temperature to the composition of the atmosphere. Any environmental changes are met with a response from living organisms. They modify the non-living part of the environment, such as the atmosphere and oceans, and all life linked to it. Like any new hypothesis, Lovelock's theory is hotly debated.

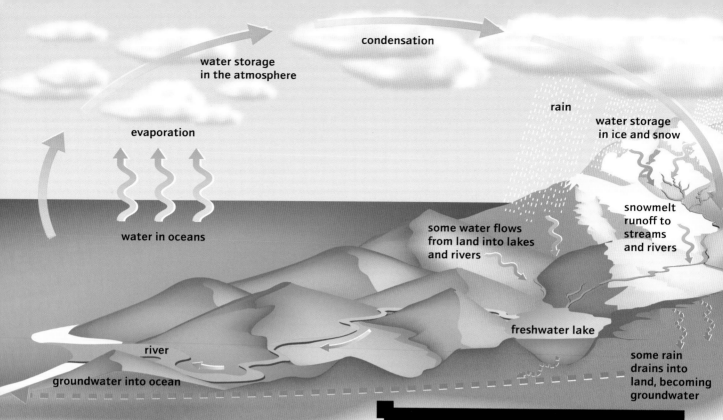

water storage
in the atmosphere

condensation

evaporation

rain

water storage
in ice and snow

water in oceans

some water flows
from land into lakes
and rivers

snowmelt
runoff to
streams
and rivers

freshwater lake

river

groundwater into ocean

some rain
drains into
land, becoming
groundwater

Water is essential for life on Earth. The water or hydrological cycle shows its continual movement on, above, and below Earth's surface.

Cycles and flows

There are two basic processes operating in any ecosystem—**energy flow** and **chemical cycling**. Several natural cycles affect living organisms, including oxygen, nitrogen, sulphur, potassium, phosphor, carbon, and water cycles. These are fueled by energy from the sun.

Carbon cycle

Carbon on Earth is exchanged constantly between four main reservoirs in the biosphere, lithosphere, hydrosphere, and atmosphere.

- In the atmosphere, carbon is mainly in the form of carbon dioxide or methane.
- In the **terrestrial** biosphere, carbon is locked up as organic carbon in the bodies of plants, animals, and micro-organisms, and in the soil.
- In the ocean, carbon is mainly in the form of dissolved bicarbonates or is found in the bodies of living or dead marine organisms.

- Carbon is trapped in the rocks of Earth, especially in coal or oil (so-called **fossil fuels**) deposits and in limestone.

Pathways exchange carbon between the four reservoirs. Plants, for example, take carbon dioxide from the atmosphere and convert it into sugars and starches during **photosynthesis**. The carbon is then stored in the fabric of the plant, part of the biosphere. This means that tropical forests are important reservoirs of carbon. If the trees are burned, carbon passes from the biosphere back to the atmosphere. Similarly, if fossil fuels are burned carbon is returned to the atmosphere as carbon dioxide.

Water cycle

Earth's water is always on the move. The sun heats the ocean and causes water to evaporate into the atmosphere, where it remains on average for nine days. During transpiration (the evaporation of water mainly from the leaves of plants), plants give off water vapor. Rising, warm air currents carry the water vapor aloft. When it cools, it condenses as tiny water droplets on dust particles to form clouds. Winds carry the clouds around the globe before the clouds drop their load of water as rain or snow. On land, gravity takes some of the water through rivers to the sea or to lakes. Some water is retained in the soil or stored in the rocks in **aquifers**. Eventually, water is returned to the ocean where the cycle continues.

EARTH'S NATURAL WATER STORAGE

Reservoir	Percentage
Oceans	97.25
Ice caps and glaciers	2.05
Groundwater	0.68
Lakes	0.01
Soil	0.005
Atmosphere	0.001
Rivers	0.0001
Biosphere	0.00004

▲ *This table shows the percentage of water stored in Earth's natural reservoirs.*

CARBON DIOXIDE AND THE GREENHOUSE EFFECT

If too much carbon dioxide ends up in the atmosphere it causes global warming. This is because carbon dioxide is a greenhouse gas. It absorbs heat coming from the Earth's surface, which has been warmed by the sun. This raises the atmospheric temperature all over the world.

Water can be stored in natural reservoirs. The largest reservoir is the ocean, where a droplet of water could remain for more than 3,000 years before moving to the next stage in the cycle. The next largest reservoir is water locked away for up to hundreds, if not thousands, of years in ice caps and glaciers. Deep groundwater can be stored for 10,000 years. A very small amount is stored in the bodies of plants and animals for as long as they live.

A ring-tailed lemur warms itself in the sun in the early morning. Energy from the sun is vital for most (but not all) of life on Earth.

The sperm whale is a secondary consumer and one of the top animals in its food chain. Except for humans, the killer whale or orca is its main predator.

Producers and consumers

Living organisms in an ecosystem rely on each other for food. There are **producers** such as green plants that produce their own food through photosynthesis, and there are **primary consumers** such as the herbivores that eat them. **Secondary consumers** such as carnivores eat the primary consumers. A simple food chain is formed when a producer (e.g. grass) is eaten by a primary consumer (zebra), which in turn is eaten by a secondary consumer (lion). The energy flow is from the producer through the primary consumer to the secondary consumer. The chain usually starts with a green plant (but not always— see pages 12 and 13) and always ends with a predator.

Food chains tend to be very short, usually no more than four steps, since energy is lost at each step in the chain. The lion, for example, has to breathe, which uses energy. It also has to stalk, ambush, and chase the zebra, which uses even more energy. This also means there are fewer animals at the top of the food chain than at the bottom. Thus, there are more plants that zebras eat than there are zebras, and more zebras that lions eat than lions. This is a simple food chain, but since animals eat more than one food it is more accurate to draw up a series of interconnecting food chains, known as a food web.

Concentrating pollutants

Remote areas of the world, such as the Arctic, are experiencing rising levels of persistent organic pollutants (POPs), even though the areas are thousands of miles from the nearest factories. The POPs are blown as air pollutants from industrial areas into the Arctic wilderness, including the Arctic Ocean. The POPs then enter the food web, becoming concentrated at every level.

In the Arctic, for example, countless planktonic organisms absorb the POPs from the water and then store them in their tiny bodies. Small fish eat huge quantities of **plankton**, and each planktonic organism they consume passes on its tiny amount of POPs. Larger fish eat many smaller fish, and each of the smaller fish passes on its load of POPs. The large fish pass on their load of POPs to seals and by the time the food chain reaches the polar bear the POPs are reaching hazardous levels. This demonstrates how a barely perceptible change in an ecosystem can have a dramatic and unexpected impact on animals living at the top of a food web.

Zooplankton or animal plankton, such as copepods, are primary consumers near the bottom of the food chain, while the small, round, multicellular algae are primary producers.

ANTARCTIC FOOD WEB

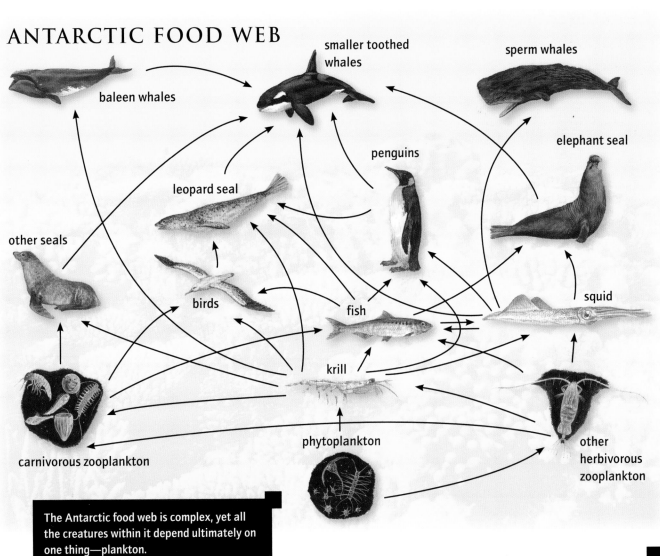

The Antarctic food web is complex, yet all the creatures within it depend ultimately on one thing—plankton.

The bright red gills of the vent tubeworm absorb sulfides and oxygen from the vent waters. This is to supply symbiotic bacteria living inside the worm with the raw materials to manufacture the food.

Unexpected energy

All living organisms require energy to live. In most living systems the ultimate source of that energy is the sun. The sun's energy is used by plants during photosynthesis and then passed from one consumer to the next in the food chain or web. There are, however, some ecosystems that do not rely on the sun.

Deep-sea hydrothermal vents

There are animal communities living in and around hot springs at the bottom of the deep sea, known as **hydrothermal vents**, which rely on energy from the Earth itself. The vents spew out mineral-rich water at a temperature of 750°F (400°C). The primary producers are chemosynthetic bacteria that turn hydrogen sulphide and iron monosulphide in the vent water into the organic materials that feed the rest of the community. This includes 6.5 ft. (2 m) long red tubeworms, giant clams and mussels, spider crabs, squat lobsters, blind shrimps, and eels. Groups of 5 in. (13 cm) long Pompeii worms have their heads in water at 72°F (22°C), yet their tails are in water at 176°F (80°C). The entire community lives without the sun. They have been found in most of the world's oceans.

Cold seeps

A very different deep-sea community lives where hydrogen sulphide, methane, and other chemicals that occur naturally in sediments at the bottom of the sea flow slowly from the sea floor at **cold seeps** or vents. Bacteria are at the base of the food chain, and since the vents last much longer than hydrothermal vents, the community of animals that relies on them grows slowly and is extremely long-lived. A seep tubeworm, for example, is believed to live for 250 years. There are also soft corals, mollusks, anemones, and crabs. There are cold seeps near Monterey on the west coast of the United States and in the Gulf of Mexico.

Brine pools

Another unusual deep-sea community is found in **brine** pools, areas of extremely dense salty water (four times as salty as the surrounding seawater) at the bottom of the sea. Thick colonies of mussels live at the edge of the pool and appear to float in space. They have a **symbiotic relationship** with a bacterium that lives in their gills and supplies them with all the food they need. They live at a depth of 2,300 ft. (700 m) in the Gulf of Mexico.

METHANE HYDRATE ICE

A recent discovery is a polychaete worm that makes its home on mounds of solid methane hydrate ice oozing from the deep sea floor. The worms are 1–2 in. (2.5–5 cm) long and they cover the mounds. Whether they depend on the methane hydrate for food is unknown. They are found about 150 miles (241 km) to the south of New Orleans in the Gulf of Mexico.

Scale worms can be found clambering among the giant tubeworms and mussels that live close to deep-sea hydrothermal vents.

ANCIENT CHANGES

Tracking change

Data on past climate change is obtained from many sources.

- Ice core samples taken from ice sheets and glaciers reveal the composition of recent past atmospheres. Chemicals from these past atmospheres are trapped in the ice and can be measured. This can show, for example, the presence or absence of greenhouse gases such as carbon dioxide and methane.
- Like ice core samples, boreholes in rock and ocean sediments give information about much earlier climate change.
- Pollen remains in lake sediments or rocks indicate the types of vegetation that were growing at different times in the past and, therefore, what the climate might have been.
- Fossils of plants and animals help build a picture of past climate, since some species lived only where specific conditions prevailed.
- Observations of Earth's orbit also contribute to climate studies (see opposite).

Drivers of past climate change

Cyclical changes in Earth's tilt and **precession**, as well as the shape (eccentricity) of Earth's orbit around the sun and the tilt of its

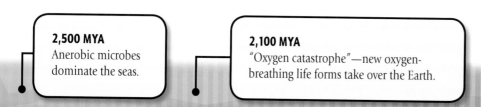

2,500 MYA
Anerobic microbes dominate the seas.

2,100 MYA
"Oxygen catastrophe"—new oxygen-breathing life forms take over the Earth.

| 2,500 MYA | 2,000 MYA | 1,500 MYA |

MYA = million years ago

rotational axis, determine how much sunlight reaches the planet's surface. Changes in eccentricity occur every 100,000 years, changes in tilt every 41,000 years, and changes in precession every 19,000–23,000 years. These changes in orbit, according to Serbian mathematician Milutin Milankovitch (1879–1958), contribute to long-term climate change, such as the appearance and disappearance of Ice Ages on Earth.

Changes within the sun determine the intensity of sunlight reaching Earth, and this causes the planet to warm up or cool down. The heating or cooling of Earth's surface disrupts ocean currents, which play an important role in distributing heat around the planet. In this way, changes in ocean currents can result in variations in climate in different parts of the world. In the North Atlantic, for example, the Gulf Stream helps boost the temperature of the British Isles.

Erupting volcanoes send airborne liquid droplets and solid particles (known as **aerosols**) into the air. The tops of volcanic clouds reflect sunlight back into space, causing short-term changes to the climate. In 1815, for example, the violent eruption of Tambora in Indonesia lowered global temperatures by 5°F (3°C), and historical accounts describe 1816 as the "year without summer." The contribution of volcanoes to carbon dioxide levels in the

atmosphere was greater in the past than it is today. Currently it is estimated that human-made carbon dioxide emissions are 130 times greater than those made by volcanic eruptions.

The angle of Earth's axis (top left) varies between 22.1° and 24.5° and is currently 23.5°. As the tilt increases, summers and winters are more extreme. Precession (top right) is the change in orientation of Earth's axis. It results in one hemisphere experiencing more extreme seasons than the other hemisphere. Earth's orbit around the sun varies between circular (bottom left) and elliptical (bottom right) during the course of 100,000 years.

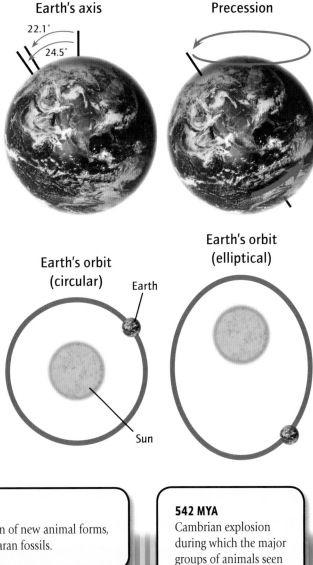

Earth's axis

22.1°
24.5°

Precession

Earth's orbit (circular)

Earth

Sun

Earth's orbit (elliptical)

830 MYA
"Snowball" or "slushball Earth" may have seen the planet mostly covered with ice.

575 MYA
Avalon explosion of new animal forms, known as Ediacaran fossils.

542 MYA
Cambrian explosion during which the major groups of animals seen today evolved.

| 1,000 MYA | 500 MYA | 1 MYA

Changes in ancient Earth

Extraordinary changes took place in the environment of the primitive Earth, and oxygen was the key element in determining the fortunes of the earliest life forms.

Roughly 2.5 billion years ago, anerobic organisms—those that do not breathe oxygen—dominated the seas. At that time there was little or no oxygen in the atmosphere. Then photosynthetic organisms appeared, such as cyanobacteria or blue-green algae, and they produced oxygen as a byproduct of photosynthesis. At first these organisms had little impact on the composition of the atmosphere, but according to David Catling, from the NASA Ames Research Center, other microbes were able to separate the hydrogen and oxygen in water. The hydrogen was lost in space while the oxygen was left behind and gradually flooded the atmosphere. Catling's ideas are based on theoretical models, but Ames researcher Tori Hoehler and his team looked at similar organisms alive today. They measured gases given off by closely-related modern **microbial mats** under conditions that simulated the early Earth. They discovered that the microbes pumped out large quantities of hydrogen at night, just as Catling's theoretical model suggested.

This is what "snowball Earth" might have looked like from space. Ice sheets covered not just the poles but also much of the planet.

The oxygen catastrophe

The increase in oxygen during the next 500 million years changed life on Earth dramatically. Roughly 2.1 billion years ago, oxygen levels reached a critical point, poisoning many of the anerobic organisms in what has been called the "oxygen catastrophe."

However, this provided opportunity for new life forms to take over, such as the eukaryotes. These differed from the earlier organisms in having cells organized into complex structures with internal membranes and a cellular skeleton, including a nucleus. Their appearance marked the beginning of much of life on Earth that exists today.

"Snowball Earth"

Roughly 830 million years ago, when the most severe Ice Age gripped the planet, another dramatic event is believed to have influenced the course of life on Earth. Some scientists believe that Earth was entirely covered in an ice sheet, up to 2,000 ft. (600 m) thick, for a period of roughly 10 million years. This event is known as "snowball Earth," though the theory itself remains controversial. While the glaciation is not disputed by geologists, the extent of the glaciation is. Some prefer to call the period "slushball Earth," in which an ice-free band occurred around the equator. However, scientists do agree that ice cover during this period ravaged the new ecosystems that depended on sunlight to photosynthesize. With photosynthesis curtailed, the composition of the atmosphere changed again. There was less oxygen and a build up of greenhouse gases,

such as carbon dioxide, which probably caused the period of global warming that followed. The ice melted, giving rise to a period of intense diversification of living organisms.

Some 575 million years ago, climate change and increasing oxygen levels were accompanied by the evolution of multicellular animals. There were segmented worm-like creatures, disc-like organisms with stripes, and plant-like **fronds**, but they looked like nothing else on Earth. These Ediacaran animals resembled none of the animals alive today.

Colorful bacteria growing in the hot springs of Yellowstone National Park, in the United States, resemble the ancient life forms that dominated the early planet.

Changes on planet Earth

While changes in the composition of the atmosphere influenced the evolution of Earth's earliest life forms, the movement of the continents, climate change, and rising and falling sea levels contributed to later large-scale environmental changes. During the past 2 billion years, Earth's climate has ranged from very cold to very hot, as well as being everything in between.

The Cambrian explosion

Little is known about climate and vegetation during the Cambrian period (c.542–488.3 million years ago), but it is believed to have been relatively warm during this time. These conditions favored the sudden diversification of life forms, known as the Cambrian explosion. All the animal **phyla** present today appeared first during the Cambrian period, including the first true **vertebrates**. Sea levels had risen, drowning the smaller landmasses. The largest landmass was the supercontinent Gondwana (a landmass with several continents joined together) that had formed at the South Pole.

At the end of the Cambrian, about 488 million years ago, a mass extinction event (in which many organisms became extinct at the same time) eliminated nearly half of the world's species, including many species of trilobites, brachiopods, and conodonts. Glaciation has been suggested as a cause, as has depletion of oxygen in the sea.

Ordovician

The Ordovician period (c.488–443.7 million years ago) followed the Cambrian and started out mild. Warm shallow seas separated the main continents of Gondwana, Laurentia, Baltica, and Siberia. Marine animals with calcium shells proliferated and there was a second period when many new species evolved. The marine fauna increased fourfold. Coral reefs appeared for the first time, as did the first bryozoans (moss animals). Graptolites (tiny animals that either floated in the sea or lived on the seabed) thrived in the oceans, and the first jawed fish evolved. However, by the late Ordovician period there was a marked change. It was one of the coldest periods in Earth's history and much of Gondwana was covered by ice. At the end of the Ordovician, about 443 million years ago, another mass extinction event occurred (see right).

Silurian

During the Silurian period (c.443.7–416 million years ago) the continents started to collide. The climate was generally warm as the world went into an extended greenhouse (warming up) phase. Southern **hemisphere** glaciers retreated and disappeared altogether. Coral reefs proliferated in the warm, shallow seas. Bony fishes covered with bony plates and functional jaws—the placoderms—evolved. Giant sea scorpions were the top marine predators.

Large quantities of broken shells found as fossils in Silurian rocks indicate that the warm surface water generated violent hurricane-like storms. The storms pounded beaches and the shallow sea floor so that shellfish were pulverized. The land began to turn green as plants took root. Mosses and liverworts **colonized** lands bordering streams. The first freshwater fish appeared, as did the first **vascular** or higher plants (plants with tissues that carry water and minerals). The Silurian period ended with a series of minor extinction events.

ORDOVICIAN MASS EXTINCTION

The extinction event at the end of the Ordovician period could have had an extraterrestrial origin. Bruce Lieberman, from the University of Kansas, proposes that a 10-second burst of **gamma rays** from a source at a distance of 6,000 **light years** hit Earth. It could have stripped away half of the **ozone layer** and exposed terrestrial and shallow water fauna to harmful **ultraviolet radiation**. This event wiped out 60 percent of marine **genera**.

Devonian

It was hot during the Devonian period (c.416–359.2 million years ago). Coral reefs were prevalent, but the seas between continents were closing and the large landmasses joined together. Lush forests with the first seed-bearing plants grew in tropical conditions on lands close to the equator. The oldest known trees appeared. Lobed-fin fishes were developing legs and making excursions out of the water, and primitive insects and spiders began to colonize the land. In the sea, sharks were evolving into top predators and **ammonites** appeared. By the late Devonian period, the supercontinent Pangea was forming. The greening of the continents, however, soaked up the carbon dioxide and the greenhouse effect was less pronounced. This caused a cooling of the climate and two examples of mass extinctions. Many jawless fish species and the placoderms disappeared. Freshwater species, including the rapidly evolving tetrapods (vertebrate animals with four limbs) were unaffected.

PERMIAN MASS EXTINCTION

Many theories have been put forward to explain why most of life on Earth disappeared at the end of the Permian period. The mass extinction had two phases, each separated by more than a million years. The current theory is that greenhouse gases built up in the atmosphere and hydrogen sulfide poisoned the seas. However, volcanic eruptions also coincided with a period of intense global warming at the end of the Permian.

Dragonflies, with a 24 in. (60 cm) wingspan, and early amphibians thrived in the tropical swamp forests during the Carboniferous period.

This 400 mile- (643 km-) long limestone fossil reef in the Guadalupe Mountains, in the southwestern United States, formed more than 250 million years ago during the Permian period.

Carboniferous

During the Carboniferous period (c.359.2–299 million years ago), extensive tropical swamp forests grew on either side of the equator in Pangea. The first conifer trees appeared. Primitive amphibians began making their way out of the oxygen-poor waters in these Carboniferous swamps. Rivers and lakes were home to the largest known freshwater fish, *Rhizodus*, which was 23 ft. (7 m) long. The forests were sandwiched between areas of desert in the north and south. An ice cap formed at the South Pole and glaciers covered what is now the Amazon Basin. A drop in sea level in the mid-Carboniferous period resulted in the extinction of many crinoids (sea lilies) and ammonites. The climate cooled at the end of the Carboniferous period.

Permian

At the start of the Permian period (c. 299–251 million years ago), much of the southern hemisphere was in the grip of an Ice Age, but tropical and temperate forests on the supercontinent Pangea still flourished in warm interglacial periods. During the middle Permian period, desert replaced the forests and reptiles spread across the entire continent. The first large herbivores and carnivores walked on land. In the beginning, these were large amphibians and pelycosaurs, or mammal-like reptiles, such as *Dimetrodon*, but later the archosaurs (that gave rise to the dinosaurs) took over. The Permian period ended with the most devastating mass extinction event in Earth's history—60–90 percent of marine species became extinct and life on Earth was almost wiped out.

Triassic

By the Triassic period (c.251–199.6 million years ago) the climate had warmed up considerably. Plants and animals diversified after the mass extinction, filling all the habitats that had been left vacant by the extinct plants and animals. The middle of Pangea was hot and dry, and warm conditions extended to the Poles. It was the hottest and driest time in the planet's history. The global average temperature was 72°F (22°C), compared to a global annual temperature during the past couple of decades of about 59°F (15°C). The first dinosaurs—plesiosaurs, ichthyosaurs, and pterosaurs—evolved, along with the first crocodiles and turtles.

The Triassic period ended with a mass extinction, and about 23 percent of families of land and marine animals died out. Though many marine reptiles disappeared, the plesiosaurs and ichthyosaurs survived. One of the greatest known volcanic eruptions occurred at about this time, but meteorite impact, cooling of the climate, and the break up of Pangea have all been proposed as having contributed. The dinosaurs filled many of the vacant niches.

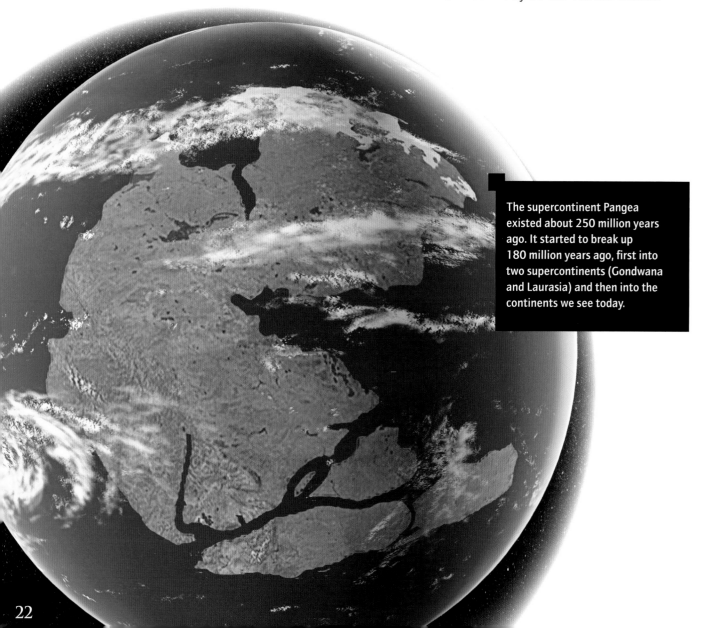

The supercontinent Pangea existed about 250 million years ago. It started to break up 180 million years ago, first into two supercontinents (Gondwana and Laurasia) and then into the continents we see today.

Jurassic and Cretaceous

The interior of Pangea was still hot and dry at first, but as Pangea broke apart the deserts started to become green. Winter ice and snow appeared at the poles during the Jurassic period (c.199.6–145.5 million years ago), but the early Cretaceous (c. 145.5–65.95 million years ago) was mild. It was the Age of the Dinosaurs.

The Jurassic was the golden age of the giant sauropods such as *Diplodocus* and *Supersaurus*. Many sauropods grew to more than 65 ft. (20 m) long and weighed more than 20 tons (20,320 kg). They fed on ferns, cycads, and conifers. Theropod dinosaurs such as *Tyrannosaurus* preyed upon them. Pterosaurs (the first reptiles to evolve flight) ruled the skies, and birds were beginning to appear.

By the Cretaceous period, Pangea had broken into the continents that exist today. After a cool start, temperatures increased and steadied, a trend maintained by volcanic activity and the release of carbon dioxide. Winds dropped and the oceans stagnated due to low oxygen levels. On land, mammals were small. Dinosaurs were at their most diverse, but the pterosaurs were beginning to be affected by competition from the evolving birds. The oldest known ants, termites, grasshoppers, and butterflies appeared. Mosasaurs, large reptilian predators, dominated the seas in the late Cretaceous period, but shark populations were on the increase.

Animal communities went into decline at the end of the Cretaceous period and then every living thing was hit by multiple catastrophic events about 65 million years ago. Plants that photosynthesize, such as phytoplankton and green land plants, declined because less solar energy reached the Earth's surface. This is believed to be due to dust in the atmosphere from either an impact by an extraterrestrial object or from erupting volcanoes. During this extinction event, the herbivores and the top predators died out. Ammonites and their principle predators, the mosasaurs, became extinct. All the non-avian dinosaurs disappeared. Insect-eaters, scavengers, and animals with a general diet survived. With such rampant death and destruction, scavengers had plenty to eat for a short time.

GREENHOUSE GASES

The warming up or cooling down of the planet can change the concentration of greenhouse gases in the atmosphere. As global temperatures rise, for example, carbon dioxide is released from the oceans. So, the warm period following an Ice Age might be caused initially by the Earth being warmed more by the sun due to the Earth's wobble, but this warming effect is increased because extra carbon dioxide enters the atmosphere from the oceans. If the planet cools, the opposite is true.

Scientists have found evidence to support this view. According to records covering the past 650,000 years, the level of carbon dioxide in the atmosphere coincides with glacial cycles. During interglacial periods (warm spells within an Ice Age) levels of carbon dioxide are high, and during cool glacial periods levels of carbon dioxide are low.

Cenozoic

The Cenozoic geological period started c.65.95 million years ago and it continues today. During this time the continents moved to their present positions. It has been a period of long-term cooling, although there was a warm period during the Miocene (c.23.03–5.33 million years ago). The Cenozoic has been called the "age of new life." Mammals diversified into a huge number of different terrestrial, flying, and marine animals. Birds had already filled the places left vacant by the pterosaurs and went on to find new, previously unexploited niches by co-adapting with the plants. Flowers and insects evolved so that one was dependent on the other—a process known as co-evolution.

At the end of the Eocene period, about 33.9 million years ago, a mass extinction event known as the "*grande coupure,*" or "great break," occurred, when mammal species underwent an abrupt change at about the same time as the first of the most recent Ice Ages. Another extinction event, the Miocene disruption, occurred about 14.5 million years ago when 30 percent of mammal genera became extinct. A crater of the same age has been found in Germany, but the event also coincides with volcanic activity in the Great African Rift Valley.

Roughly 3 million years ago, in the Pliocene (c.5.33–2.59 million years ago), an Arctic ice cap formed. Around this time the first recognizable human appeared in Africa and the Isthmus of Panama formed, allowing an interchange of species between North and South America.

ICE AGE

The most recent period of glaciations occurred roughly 2.59 million years ago. However, it was not freezing all the time, and periods of intense cold were punctuated by warm interglacial periods. During the middle of the Ice Age, for example, lions, hyenas, and hippopotamuses lived in the area that is now London. The early humans adapted to these changing conditions. They thrived in the warm periods and during the cold periods they adapted to the icy conditions by living in caves, making clothes, and using fire to keep warm. By the Holocene period, which started at the end of the last Ice Age about 11,000 years ago, humans had come to dominate the planet.

The concept of time is mind-boggling. Geological time was first recognized in the 11th century by Chinese scientist and statesman Shen Kuo, and independently in the 1700s by the Scottish geologist James Hutton. They both recognized that Earth has had an extremely long history, between 4 and 5 billion years. Scientists now speak of events that happened millions, hundreds of millions, and even billions of years ago. These periods of time are hard to imagine, so they have been organized into units. The largest unit is the Supereon. This is divided into Eons and these are divided into Periods, Epochs, and Stages (or Ages). Geologists divide these units further into Lower, Middle, and Upper, which refers to the rocks themselves, and Early, Middle, or Late, which refers to the time. Stages (or Ages) tend to be regional and are often classified by the fossils they contain, so a Stage on one continent might have a different name on another continent. ▶

GEOLOGICAL TIMELINE

Eons and Times	Eras	Periods	Epochs	Years	Events
Phanerozoic	Cenozoic	Quaternary	Holocene	Today–11,430 years ago	Holocene extinction. Age of humans.
			Pleistocene	11,430 years ago–2.59 MYA	Saber-toothed cats and mammoths.
		Tertiary	Pliocene	2.59–5.33 MYA	Hominids (human ancestors), many whales, and *Megalodon* shark.
			Miocene	5.33–23.03 MYA	Horses, dogs, bears, modern birds.
			Oligocene	23.03–33.9 MYA	Rhinos, deer, pigs.
			Eocene	33.9–55.8 MYA	Rodents, whales.
			Paleocene	55.8–65.95 MYA	Large mammals and primitive primates.
	Mesozoic	Cretaceous		65.95–145.5 MYA	Cretaceous-Tertiary extinctions. Marsupials, snakes, crocodiles, bees, butterflies, flowering plants.
		Jurassic		145.5–199.6 MYA	Birds, pterosaurs. Age of the dinosaurs begins.
		Triassic		199.6–251 MYA	Triassic-Jurassic extinctions. Mammals, ichthyosaurs, dinosaurs.
	Paleozoic	Permian		251–299 MYA	Permian mass extinctions. Age of amphibians.
		Carboniferous		299–359.2 MYA	Reptiles, winged insects, conifers. Golden age of sharks.
		Devonian		359.2–416 MYA	Late-Devonian extinctions. Amphibians, sharks, club mosses, horsetails, and ferns. Age of fishes.
		Silurian		416–443.7 MYA	Vascular plants, jawed fish.
		Ordovician		443.7–488.3 MYA	Ordovician-Silurian extinctions. Land plants, corals.
		Cambrian		488.3–542 MYA	Jawless fishes, vertebrates. Age of trilobites. Cambrian explosion —today's major groups of animals or phyla appear.
Precambrian time	Proterozoic			542–2,500 MYA	Sponges appear. Multicellular life.
	Archaean			2,500–3,800 MYA	Blue-green algae and bacteria. Life forms in sea.
	Hadean			3,800–4,570 MYA	Earth's crust solidifies.

Earth, together with the rest of the solar system, was formed about 4.56–4.57 billion years ago.

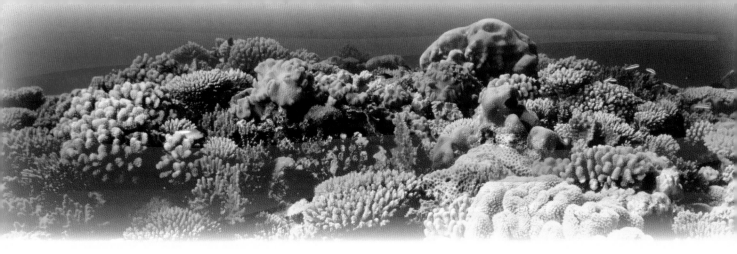

RECENT GLOBAL
CHANGES

Today, Earth remains in an Ice Age. Three large ice sheets exist in Greenland, southern South America, and Antarctica. Ice cover is not as extensive as it was at the climax of the last Ice Age phase, about 15,000 years ago. Then, giant ice sheets 2–3 miles (3–5 km) thick covered the northern parts of North America, Europe, and Asia. Their southernmost edge was in the middle of what is now London and Long Island.

Glacials and interglacials

The most recent Ice Age started roughly 40 million years ago, when an ice sheet appeared in the Antarctic. It intensified in three steps about 36, 15, and 3 million years ago. During the last phase, ice sheets spread across the northern hemisphere, but they were not permanent. They advanced and retreated more than 20 times, creating cold, dry glacial periods and warm, wet interglacial periods. During glacial periods sea levels dropped and ocean circulation was disrupted. More sunlight was reflected away from the planet due to an increase in snow and ice, reduced forest cover, and a reduction in the amount of open water. Levels of greenhouse gases in the atmosphere dropped at the onset of glacial periods and increased in interglacial periods. During interglacial periods, sea levels rose

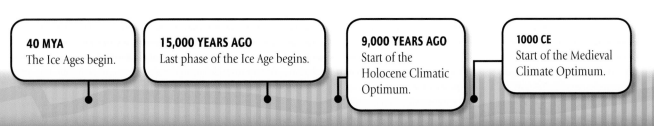

40 MYA
The Ice Ages begin.

15,000 YEARS AGO
Last phase of the Ice Age begins.

9,000 YEARS AGO
Start of the Holocene Climatic Optimum.

1000 CE
Start of the Medieval Climate Optimum.

| 50 MYA | 15,000 years ago | 1000 CE |

MYA = million years ago

and almost tropical conditions were established. Hippopotamus and crocodile remains have been found in sediments below Trafalgar Square, London.

The great exchange

During glacial periods, organisms used to the cold were pushed south into lower latitudes, and organisms that preferred warm conditions were squeezed into areas closer to the equator or became extinct. In the lands south of the ice sheets, large cold-adapted mammalian species, such as the woolly mammoth and woolly rhinoceros, evolved. Giant beavers were the size of black bears. Dire wolves, short-faced bears, and saber-toothed cats hunted down the giant herbivores. The dropping sea level exposed land bridges between North and South America and between North America and Asia, resulting in a great exchange of animals between the continents. Competition for habitats was fierce. It was during this period of change in Earth's history that modern humans evolved.

GORILLA REFUGIA

During the last Ice Age, cold, dry conditions prevailed south of the ice sheets. This led to the contraction of tropical forests. Only isolated patches, or refugia, survived. Gorillas were confined to these refugia, which were separated from each other by major rivers. Gorillas do not cross large rivers, so each gorilla population evolved independently of others. Today, this is reflected in the genetic makeup of gorillas—animals from different regions have significantly different **genes**.

The Portage Glacier in Alaska has retreated substantially in recent years, but it still shows that Earth is in the grip of an Ice Age.

1300 CE
Start of the Little Ice Age.

1789
Severe El Niño coincides with the French Revolution.

1982
Severe El Niño coincides with extensive bush fires in Australia.

| 1500 CE | 1800 | 1900 |

A "Frost Fair" taking place near London Bridge on the frozen River Thames, England, at the time of the Little Ice Age. It was painted in the year of the Great Frost (1783–1784), when the Thames froze for two months and the ice was 11 in. (28 cm) thick.

Ancient weather

Between 9,000 and 5,000 years ago, the world experienced a significant warm period known as the Holocene Climatic Optimum. The North Pole warmed up by 7°F (4°C), while further away from the poles the degree of warming was less. Africa was generally wetter. The Sahara was dotted with lakes inhabited by typical tropical African lake animals, such as crocodiles and hippopotamuses. The period ended abruptly, probably due to a change in the Earth's orbit. The Sahara became an arid desert and much of the fauna died out. Today, the few survivors are concentrated in **oases**.

Medieval weather

From the 10th–14th centuries, records show that countries bordering the North Atlantic experienced unusually warm weather. Ice-free seas meant that the Vikings could settle in Greenland and even push on to North America. Grapes for wine were grown as far north as southern Great Britain. This was a period known as the Medieval Climate Optimum. Then, starting in 1450, the temperature began to drop, with two significant dips in the 17th and 19th centuries. This period has been described as the Little Ice Age. Rivers, such as the Thames, froze over and fairs were held on the ice (see above).

In 1780, New York harbor froze and allowed people to walk between Manhattan and Staten Island. Greenland and Iceland became icebound and mountain glaciers advanced in many parts of the world. In Europe, springs and summers were cold and wet with wide-spread flooding. Food shortages resulted in bread riots and mass starvation. In the natural world, hardier oaks and pines replaced beech trees across Europe and North America. The famous Italian stringed-instrument maker Antonio Stradivari (1644–1737) made his violins during the Little Ice Age. The colder climate resulted in denser wood, which led to the rich tone of his instruments.

DESERT CROCODILES

In Mauritania, on the southern edge of the Sahara Desert, Nile crocodiles have been discovered hiding in caves, tunnels, and under rocks close to wetland areas that are dry for most of the year. Tara Shine, from the University of Ulster in Northern Ireland, found 45 isolated sites on the edge of the desert. Many of them were in guelta areas, where rainwater accumulates in clay-lined basins or underground springs create pools of water in rocky depressions. However, it can be dry for six months or more. These crocodiles are no more than 5 ft. (1.5 m) long, unlike the more usual 16 ft. (5 m) of adult Nile crocodiles. They spend the driest months relatively inactive, occasionally coming out of their refuges at night when the temperature drops. They are a **relict** population of crocodiles that once inhabited a greener Sahara.

MEDIEVAL AND LITTLE ICE AGE TEMPERATURE GRAPH

▼ *This graph shows temperatures deviating significantly from the norm (0 °C) in the Northern Hemisphere during Medieval times.*

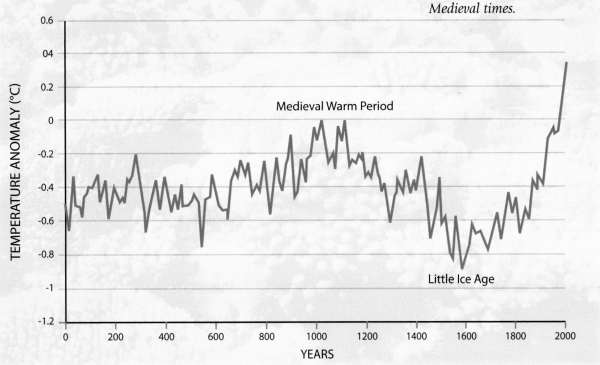

EL NIÑO

Christmas 1982 and the months that followed saw droughts, dust storms, and bush fires in Australia, Asia, and Africa. Peru received the heaviest rain in its history, with downpours of 132 in. (335 cm) in places instead of the normal 6 in. (15 cm). In California, heavy rain triggered landslides and warm seas encouraged red tides—blooms of red algae that poisoned fish and other marine creatures (see page 37). Hurricane activity increased in the North Atlantic. The sea level dropped in the western Pacific, exposing and killing coral reefs, and rose in the mid and eastern Pacific, where seabirds were forced to leave their nests. On the coast of Peru, 25 percent of adult seals and sea lions perished along with all their pups. In the same area, huge numbers of seabirds died and chicks were abandoned. The cause? El Niño.

Global chaos

El Niño is the name given to a disruption of the ocean-atmosphere system in the tropical Pacific. It not only influences

▲ *A Peruvian booby nest colony, Peru, which could be affected by El Niño.*

EL NIÑO AND THE FRENCH REVOLUTION

Scientists studying the pattern of past El Niño events have shown that an unusually strong El Niño occurred between 1789 and 1793. It gave rise to poor crop yields in Europe, resulting in high food prices and widespread famine and starvation. They suggest this particular El Niño might have contributed to the political upheaval that became the French Revolution (1789–99).

▲ *Pelagic red crab occasionally wash ashore in large numbers along the southern California coast, signaling the start of an El Niño.*

the weather in the Pacific region but also around the globe. El Niño, meaning "little boy," was named because it generally occurs around Christmas time, said to be the time of Jesus' birth. It takes place irregularly every two to seven years and can last for up to two years.

In 1982 there was an especially ferocious El Niño. The trade winds, which normally blow from east to west in the Pacific, reversed their direction. The ocean currents also changed direction. This meant that the west coast of South America, normally bathed in cold water from the Antarctic, was inundated with warm water from the equatorial Pacific.

Near the coast of Peru the sea-surface temperature shot up 7.2°F (4°C), with severe consequences. Upwellings of nutrients from the sea floor, which normally fed the blooms of plankton on which many fishes feed, stopped. This meant that important fish populations, such as hake, jack mackerel, and anchoveta, moved to deeper, cooler waters and shrimp and sardines migrated south. The seabirds that fed on these marine animals abandoned their nests and followed the fish out to sea. Chicks and any adult birds that stayed behind died of starvation. It was a natural catastrophe during which wildlife had to change its regular behavior and adapt to changing conditions or die.

Prediction

In order to prepare for the severe weather that El Niño could bring and avoid the devastation it causes, scientists are trying to predict future El Niño events. To do this, they construct prediction models based on past events and monitor ocean and atmosphere changes, such as changes in ocean speed and direction, wind speed, and sea level. Countries such as Peru are using these predictions to plan their fisheries, agriculture, and water resources.

LOCAL CHANGE

Wildfires cause change

It usually takes years or millions of years to transform an ecosystem, but wildfires can do this in a matter of days. In 1988, 36 percent of Yellowstone National Park in the United States went up in flames. At the time it seemed to be a catastrophe, yet recovery was immediate—fireweed appeared just days after the fire had passed. With the **understory** and **canopy** burned, wild flowers covered the forest floor for several years afterward. Twenty years later, acres of dead lodgepole pines still stand, but the forest did not die with them. Lodgepole pinecones need high temperatures to open and release their seeds, so the fires ensured seeds were distributed and saplings grew. Yellowstone's forests have been regenerated by fire.

Scientists generally consider wildfires to be a natural part of an ecosystem. Some plants have adaptations, such as secondary shoots or fire-resistant seeds, which enable them to survive fires. Eucalyptus trees are packed with flammable oils that fuel fires and inadvertently eliminate the competition. Some plants, such as Yellowstone's lodgepole pinecones, need fire in order to grow or reproduce.

1910
Largest fire in U.S. history burns down forests in Washington, Montana, and Idaho, killing 86 people.

1936
Russian town of Kursha-2 engulfed by wildfire and 1,200 people killed.

1988
Worst fires in Yellowstone's history eventually put out by snow.

| 1920 | 1940 | 1980 |

Brush fires and firestorms

A wildfire can be ignited naturally by lightning or volcanic eruption and artificially by human carelessness or deliberate **arson**. Fire spreads in several ways:

- through the undergrowth by "crawling";
- from tree crown to tree crown to create a firestorm;
- by "jumping" with the aid of burning leaves and branches that are lifted ahead of the fire.

As the fire burns, rising hot air draws in cooler air from the surrounding area and wind fans the flames.

Fires usually occur in the summer and fall months. Plants dry out and when under stress they produce the flammable gas ethylene. This makes for a **tinder**-dry environment that ignites and spreads fire in seconds. Some wildlife communities live with the constant threat of fire, such as the Mediterranean maquis, the veld and fynbos of South Africa, the forests and scrublands of Australia, and the forested and desert scrub areas of North America. In southern California there have been so many fires that native plant communities have almost been eliminated and introduced weeds are taking over.

SANTA ANA WINDS

In California, dry winds from the desert (known as the Santa Ana winds) move wildfires along at a rate of 40 miles (65 km) a day. In October 2003, 15 California wildfires—fanned by the Santa Ana winds—burned 1,150 sq. miles (2,980 sq km) of forest and scrub. It was the largest spate of wildfires in California's history, which became known as the 2003 Firestorm. During the same year, bush fires in Australia swept through the suburbs of the capital city, Canberra.

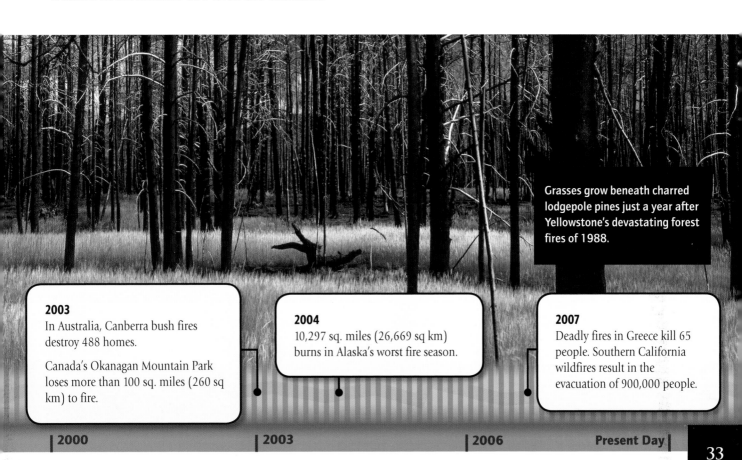

Grasses grow beneath charred lodgepole pines just a year after Yellowstone's devastating forest fires of 1988.

2003
In Australia, Canberra bush fires destroy 488 homes.

Canada's Okanagan Mountain Park loses more than 100 sq. miles (260 sq km) to fire.

2004
10,297 sq. miles (26,669 sq km) burns in Alaska's worst fire season.

2007
Deadly fires in Greece kill 65 people. Southern California wildfires result in the evacuation of 900,000 people.

| 2000 | | 2003 | | 2006 | Present Day |

Volcanic eruptions

Apart from an extraterrestrial object colliding with Earth, one of the most devastating changes to an ecosystem is a volcanic eruption. While **molten larva** and fireballs of burning gas, rock, and dust (pyroclastic flows) can ignite vegetation on its edges, the real power of the volcano is felt when it literally blows itself apart. At times like these, every living thing is obliterated and life must start again. Such a catastrophe took place in 1883 when a series of massive explosions caused the volcanic island of Krakatoa (in Indonesia) to first blow apart and then sink into the empty **magma chamber** and disappear below the waves. Three small parts of the original volcano survived as islands In 1884, when scientists briefly visited the largest island, Rakata, the only living thing they found was a spider hiding in a crevice.

Born again

In 1927, eruptions started again on the spot where the old Krakatoa had been, and Anak Krakatoa, meaning "Child of Krakatoa," rose out of the sea. Since then the island has been erupting almost continuously, with periods of intense volcanic activity interspersed with days of relative calm. Anak Krakatoa has been growing at about 5 inches (13 cm) a week. In 2008, it appeared it was becoming active again, but the most recent major eruptions were in 2007. People in boats must now be more than 2 miles (3 km) from the island.

Despite these turbulent changes, life has returned to the area. Just over a century after Krakatoa's explosions effectively wiped out life on the surviving islands, they have been re-colonized. Rakata is covered with dense

Anak Krakatoa during an uncharacteristic lull in activity. Despite the constant eruptions and covering of volcanic ash, plants and animals have re-colonized the island.

tropical forest, including 400 higher plant species, and is home to 2 ft. (60 cm) long water monitors, three species of geckos, a skink, the paradise flying snake, two species of rats, and 17 species of bats. Saltwater crocodiles make regular visits. There are 25 species of land birds breeding on the islands and another 30 species of avian visitors, as well as 54 species of butterflies and 18 species of land mollusks. And despite regularly dumping ash and volcanic debris onto its slopes, even the active volcano Anak Krakatoa is being re-colonized. Krakatoa has shown that, given time, a tropical forest ecosystem is capable of recovering from extreme damage.

North American disaster

In 1980 in southwest Washington, the volcano, Mount St. Helens, blew out its side. There was enough debris to cover a football field 150 miles high with ash and mud! Entire forests were felled by the blast, and the countless plants and animals that lived in them were killed. River waters became so hot that fish were jumping out onto dry land to avoid the heat, and 600 mph (966 kmh) furnace-like ash clouds scorched everything in their path. Yet nature recovered surprisingly quickly.

Scientists thought that plants would be the first pioneers to re-colonize the area, but they were wrong. Spiders flew in on their gossamer threads almost immediately—up to 2 million a day. Many perished, because there was little to eat, but beetles arrived to clear up their dead bodies. The first birds to return

COLONIZATION

In order to reach Anak Krakatoa the colonizers had to cross at least 27 miles (44 km) of sea from the nearest land. They traveled using one of three methods:

- by air—birds, insects, and bats could actively fly in, while orchid seeds and fern spores were blown by the wind;
- by sea—many animals, both large and small, swam or drifted in the ocean current on rafts, since the Krakatoa Islands are down current from Sumatra;
- by hitchhiking—small creatures traveled on the feet of or inside birds and seeds. Rats most likely came in boats.

were those more often seen in deserts and shrubland country, such as meadowlarks, rock wrens, and American pipits. Pocket gophers, that survived the blast in their underground burrows, began to mix up the soil. Their burrows also served as a refuge for frogs, newts, and salamanders that survived the eruption because they were in frozen ponds.

When plants finally arrived, they were species that had a symbiotic relationship in their roots with bacteria that "fix" nitrogen from the atmosphere, such as lupines. Others followed—red alder, cottonwood, and willow are now growing where there are pockets of water. Elk came to eat the leaves of those plants that had recovered. Stunted pines and firs wait for the deciduous trees to run their course before they finally take over and the forests are restored to what they once were.

Small but deadly micro-organisms

An infinitesimally small organism can have a major impact on an ecosystem. For example, a bacterium or virus responsible for a fatal disease can kill off an animal or plant that is an important link in a food chain, causing the food chain to collapse.

Animal diseases

From time to time outbreaks of rhinderpest, a viral disease of cattle, devastate herds of large African herbivores, such as buffalo, as well as domestic cattle. As the herbivores die, populations of predators such as lions, hunting dogs, and hyenas, and scavengers such as vultures and jackals, also decline as their food source dwindles. On the other hand, if a disease like distemper hits a major predator such as wild dogs or lions, then sick herbivores continue to live where previously they would have been killed by the predators. These herbivores live to infect other animals in the herd and in this way the disease quickly spreads through the population. Either way, the food web is broken.

A red tide caused by a bloom of algae changes the color of the sea off the Bountiful Islands in the Gulf of Carpentaria, Northwest Queensland, Australia. Some species of fish and marine mammals succumb to the toxins and die, while shellfish accumulate the poisons in their tissues (the source of serious food poisoning for humans).

Red tides

In the sea, certain types of microscopic **phytoplankton** can increase in numbers to such an extent that they kill other marine creatures, upsetting food web dynamics and disrupting ecosystems. The most dangerous organisms are species of red marine algae, such as the dinoflagellate *Karenia brevis*. When they increase in numbers to the extent that there are tens of millions of cells per gallon of water, they color the sea reddish-brown, hence the name "red tide." These harmful algal blooms, or HABs as they are known, produce toxins that accumulate in the food chain. The toxins disable the central nervous system of fish so they cannot breathe, resulting in huge schools of dead fish being washed up on beaches. Marine mollusks such as mussels, oysters, and clams also absorb the toxins. The shellfish are unaffected, but as they filter out the algae during their feeding process, the toxin builds up in their tissues. Larger animals eat the contaminated fish and shellfish and are either very sick or die. *Karenia* toxins, for example, are responsible for the deaths of many whales, dolphins, and manatees along the Florida coast, and people become very ill from eating contaminated shellfish.

FISH KILLER

In 1996, fish with large bloody wounds on their bodies were found in Chesapeake Bay on the east coast of the United States. Professor JoAnn Burkholder, from North Carolina State University, discovered that an especially nasty HAB organism called *Pfiesteria* was responsible. At first a toxin produced by the algae was believed to be responsible, but Bob Gawley, from the University of Miami at Coral Gables, and Wolfgang Vogelbein, from the Virginia Institute of Marine Sciences, found that the tiny algae tear strips of skin off the fish and cause large wounds that may be infected later by water mold. The stricken fish eventually die.

▲ *Here, wounds caused by the dinoflagellate alga* Pfeisteria *are clearly visible on the fish.*

A gap in the canopy of a Malaysian rain forest caused by a fallen tree has meant that sunlight reaches the floor. Plants grow rapidly in a race to fill the vacant space.

Rain forest race

Little sunlight reaches the floor of a tropical rain forest because the tree crowns close the canopy and keep light from coming though. Seeds **germinating** on the ground grow slowly or lie dormant. When a tall rain forest tree dies and falls to the ground, a hole appears in the canopy and sunlight floods in. This marks the start of a race for saplings to grow up into the gap. First in the race to grow are **pioneer** species.

Plant succession

In South and Central America, *Cecropia* species are pioneer plants from the nettle family. They grow rapidly to close a gap in the canopy, thereby creating the right conditions for the secondary growth of shade-loving trees. Climax plants such as tall kapok trees follow the *Cecropia* into the forest canopy. With the gap closed, light no longer penetrates the canopy and the light-loving plants die and leave tall rain forest trees up to 150 ft. (46 m) high. This natural progression is important when forests that have been destroyed by commercial logging are replanted. Reforestation is not just planting trees—it is creating a new forest with its great diversity of plants and animals.

DWIGHT BILLINGS
(1910–1997)

Dwight Billings was an U.S. ecologist who carried out research on **plant succession** in the 1930s. He studied how plants colonized abandoned agricultural land in North Carolina.

- Billings found that the first plants to grow on the bare ground were **annuals**. These plants grew rapidly and produced small, easily dispersed seeds, completing their life cycle in one growing season.
- Grasses and **perennial** plants that complete their life cycle in two years or more were next to appear. In just over a year these plants had dominated the vegetation.
- After three or four years herbs and shrubs appeared.
- Between 5 and 15 years after the fields had been abandoned, softwood trees (such as pines and sweetgum) started to grow. They began to form a forest canopy that shaded the ground. Light-loving herbs and shrubs were gradually replaced by shade-loving ground cover, and pine seedlings now failed to grow in the low light levels. The canopy also changed the **microclimate** close to the ground, which became more humid with less wind. A **soil litter** layer formed, allowing oak and hickory seeds, which tolerate low light conditions, to germinate.
- Some 50–75 years after the pioneering species had colonized the abandoned fields, hardwoods (such as oak) replaced the softwoods.
- After 100 years, some of the fields had become oak forests, the **climax vegetation**.

POND TO LAND

If a natural pond in North America is left to itself, it eventually becomes dry land. A succession of plants is involved in the transformation. At first, swamp loosestrife grows in the shallow water at the edge of the pond, and then sphagnum moss fills in the gaps. Soil is washed gradually from the land. Together with debris from plants growing in the pond and leaves blown in from neighboring trees, the pond itself slowly fills with debris. Blueberries and poison sumac take hold, followed by small trees such as black spruce and American larch. Finally, swamp maples and white pines grow tall, and the pond has all but disappeared.

Seasonal changes

The most obvious changes to an ecosystem take place regularly every year. In temperate regions there are four seasons (winter, spring, summer, and fall) and in the tropics there are two seasons (wet and dry). Plants and animals living in such climatic regimes are adapted to cope with the extremes, and the availability of light appears to play a leading role in how they behave.

Spring colors

There are seasons to observe even in the tropical rain forest. Trees tend to have new leaves during the dry season, the Amazon having 25 percent more leaf cover at this time of year. Unlike temperate forest trees, whose leaves turn red in fall, the leaves on rain forest trees are red when they are new and turn green as they mature. The greener forests capture more sunlight, absorb more carbon dioxide, and transpire more water. In this way the trees gradually **humidify** the atmosphere and play a role in the onset of the wet season. Lack of sunlight in the wet season limits forest growth more than lack of water in the dry season.

Spring flowers

Spring in temperate woodland in Europe marks the start of a frantic race. The trees are in bloom and leaves are about to open. The spring flowers—snowdrops, daffodils, celandines, wild garlic, and bluebells—must

The red, orange, and yellow leaves of fall are an indication that large-scale chemical changes are taking place in the trees as they prepare for winter.

grow and flower quickly before the trees' leaves obscure sunlight from the forest floor. Flowers such as the snowdrop, daffodil, and bluebell have a store of nutrients in an underground bulb to give them a head start. Snowdrops appear even while winter snow lies on the ground. This race for light produces a wonderful show of flowers each spring.

MOVING OUT AND SHUTTING DOWN

Shortening days trigger some animals to **migrate**. Birds migrate to ensure they spend the greater part of the year in conditions that are optimum for their survival by heading to places in the opposite hemisphere. Arctic terns, for example, take advantage of the long summer days at high northern latitudes before flying across the world to take advantage of the long summer days at high southern latitudes—a journey of some 11,000 miles (17,500 km). In this way the terns maximize the hours of daylight available to catch fish throughout the year. When the days shorten, some animals simply shut down, conserve energy, and wait for things to improve. As the days get shorter and food is less available, some animals **hibernate**. The hibernating animal reduces its heart and breathing rate and lowers its body temperature. While asleep, it uses its fat reserve for food. Bats, chipmunks, and ground squirrels hibernate. The only bird known to hibernate is the common poorwill of North America.

Deforestation is destroying vast tracts of tropical rain forest. With the trees go potential new medicines to fight the world's most serious diseases. This lake, in the Malaysian rain forest, formed as a result of flooding from a human-made dam. It is used to assist in the felling and logging of rain forest trees.

Human influence

Few ecosystems today are untouched by people. Human population growth, habitat fragmentation, deforestation, industry, agriculture, pollution, over-hunting, and illegal **poaching** have all impacted on wildlife communities, even in the remotest parts of the world. Human changes to ecosystems have been as significant as those brought about by natural change. These changes can be direct, such as illegal hunting, or indirect, such as pollution.

Unexpected effects

Changes to an ecosystem triggered by human activities can have unexpected effects. In 2008, Todd Palmer, from the University of Florida,

Gainsville, and colleagues published a scientific paper showing how the removal of large animals from an ecosystem, by hunting or poaching, has an impact even on the smallest animals. They fenced off an area of African savannah containing stands of whistling thorn acacia trees so that no elephants, giraffes, or other large browsers could eat the vegetation. The experiment simulated what would happen if poachers exterminated all the large animals. They discovered that populations of four species of ants, which rely on the whistling thorn tree for food and shelter, went into decline, as did the trees themselves.

The relationship between the whistling thorn acacia trees and the four species of ants was a mutually dependent arrangement. The trees provided the ants with shelter (they lived in special swollen thorns on the trees) and food (in the form of a sugary sap distributed from the base of the leaves). In return, the ants defended the trees from animals that like to eat acacia by swarming over anything that threatened the trees.

During the 10 years the trees were fenced off, however, the trees provided fewer shelters and less sap, so there were fewer ants. This allowed another ant species to invade the trees. This new species of ant encouraged wood-boring beetle larvae to attack the trees, since the ants then occupied the larvae's empty tunnels. So, with the defensive species of ants gone, the trees suffered because wood-boring beetles attacked the trees more often. The trees behind the fence

NOT WILD AT ALL

In many countries, much of the landscape is human-made. In Sweden and Finland, for example, only 5 percent of ancient forests remain and the vast tracts of forest there today are all human-made. In the British Isles, the Dorset heaths and Scottish grouse moors may appear like wilderness areas but they are actually maintained by people. Meadows filled with wild flowers may look untouched, but they are carefully manicured at key times during the year to ensure the flowers grow and bloom in profusion during the spring and summer. If left alone, the heaths, moors, and meadows would turn to **scrub**.

were twice as likely to die as those outside, and any surviving trees grew 65 percent more slowly. Palmer and his co-workers had shown that the ecological effects of removing large herbivores had been greater than previously imagined.

The Scottish grouse moors are maintained by regular burning. This allows younger shoots to grow, providing food for the valuable grouse and other moorland animals.

ADAPTATION TO CHANGE

Specialists and generalists

Specialized organisms are less able to adapt to change than generalists. Specialist animal species live in a narrow range of conditions and eat a limited diet. For example, the caterpillar of the peacock butterfly eats mainly stinging nettles and occasionally hop plants. Generalist animal species thrive in a wide range of conditions and can switch diets. Many **omnivores**, such as bears and raccoons in North America, are generalists, eating berries, eggs, fish, and meat.

Some herbivores are specialists:
- many moth and butterfly caterpillars are confined to one species of plant;
- koalas eat mainly *Eucalyptus* leaves;
- pygmy rabbits in North America survive the winter by feeding exclusively on sagebrush.

Predators can be generalists (such as praying mantises and spiders) or specialists (such as anteaters and pangolins). When conditions are good and food is plentiful, specialists can out-compete generalists.

MID-17TH CENTURY
Ox-eye daisy seeds carried in crop seed sacks by European colonists to North America—eventually to grow in 50 U.S. states.

1788
Rabbits introduced to Australia. They destroy the landscape to such an extent that native species are wiped out.

MID-19TH CENTURY
Japanese knotweed introduced from Far East to Europe and North America. It quickly dominates many sheltered valleys, gardens, and abandoned sites.

1600   1700   1800

However, if conditions change, specialists are more likely to become extinct than generalists. In Yellowstone National Park, for example, mule deer are specialists that rely on sagebrush for their winter feed, but elk, who are generalists, have also started to feed on the shrub. This has increased competition for sagebrush, resulting in a decline in the number of sagebrush plants and consequently a decline in the number of mule deer.

Invasive generalists

Plants can be specialists living within a narrow range of conditions or generalists and grow just about anywhere. Cactuses tend to be specialists, adapted to grow in hot and dry places. Weeds, such as dandelions, tend to be generalists.

Invasive plant species, such as Japanese knotweed that has overrun many parts of the United Kingdom, are also generalists. Knotweed is successful because it relies on rhizomes—underground stems—for reproduction. They spread up to 23 ft. (7 m) from the parent plant. The tiniest pieces of the plant, which are easily carried away by streams or when they stick to the side of a vehicle, can grow into a new knotweed plant. Knotweed leaf litter is also poisonous to native plants, so wherever knotweed grows it soon dominates the landscape. In this way, and with a little help from people who have carried the plant around the world, Japanese knotweed has become a global pest.

Adapting to humans

Black rats and brown rats are born survivors. The secret of their success is to live wherever humans live. But, in the absence of people, they can live just about anywhere and eat just about anything. Animal behavior researcher Martin Schein, from Pennsylvania State University, studied the diet of brown rats, looking at what rats pick out of household garbage. He discovered their favorite food is scrambled eggs, macaroni and cheese was a close second, with cooked corn third. Their least liked food turned out to be raw celery or beets, and peaches.

Invasive Japanese knotweed presents an almost impenetrable wall to a pest control operative in Cornwall, United Kingdom.

1876
Kudzu vine from Japan imported into United States smothers other plants.

1884
Water hyacinth brought to the United States from Brazil—soon clogs water courses from Florida to California.

1935
Cane toad introduced to Australia as part of a pest control program, but it quickly becomes a pest itself.

1946
Paper bark trees brought from Australia to the United States. Soon, they have taken over parts of the Everglades swamps like "living walls."

| 1850 | 1900 | 1950 |

MICE AND RAT INFESTATIONS

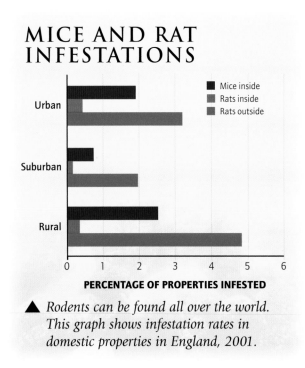

Legend:
- Mice inside
- Rats inside
- Rats outside

Categories (top to bottom): Urban, Suburban, Rural

X-axis: PERCENTAGE OF PROPERTIES INFESTED (0 to 6)

▲ *Rodents can be found all over the world. This graph shows infestation rates in domestic properties in England, 2001.*

Rats are generalists, living wherever they can find space and eating almost anything they find. Brown rats originated in northern China, but today they are found on every continent except Antarctica. It is said that in the city you are no more than a few feet away from a rat, though it depends on the city—cities with cold winters, such as New York, have fewer rats than cities with warmer winters, such as London. In 2003, the National Rodent Survey of the United Kingdom revealed a population of 60 million rats in the country, the same as its human population!

Bug survivors

Like rats, cockroaches are able to adapt to tough conditions. Of the 4,300 known species, just 30 live in the same places as people and have become pests. Cockroaches live everywhere except polar regions and altitudes above 6,500 ft. (2,000 m). They also have a long history. Fossils of cockroach-like insects have been found in rocks 315 million years old.

AUTOMOBILE DISPERSAL

Automobiles and trucks are effective seed dispersers for many roadside plants. In a study by Nigel Wace (1929–2005) in Canberra, Australia, the wastewater from a car wash facility was filtered for seeds and the seeds were planted for a period of 26 months. Of the 18,500 seeds germinated, the researchers found 259 species of plants. Twenty species were not from the area and had traveled long distances. Coastal species had been carried at least 100 miles (160 km). With so many vehicles moving on roads around the world, road systems are believed to be important agents in the mixing of plant species.

▼ *The graph below shows the source of plant seedlings and species found in an urban car wash in Canberra, Australia.*

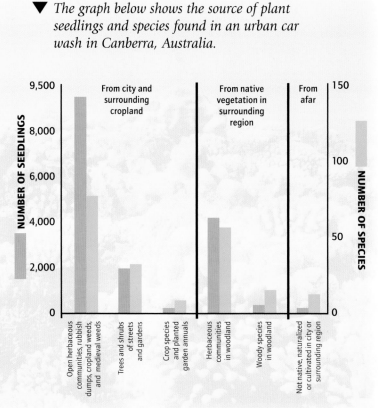

It is often said that cockroaches will survive on Earth when people have gone, even after a nuclear holocaust. In fact, cockroaches are nearly as intolerant of radiation as people. Roughly 90 percent of humans are killed by 1,200 **rads**, whereas cockroaches are killed by 6,400 rads. Even fruit flies are still alive up to 64,000 rads. The real survivor, however, is the bacterium *Deinococcus radiodurans*. It survives 1,500,000 rads and twice as much if frozen!

Life, as we have seen, is extraordinarily resilient, and evolution ensures that it remains that way. The healthiest organisms survive, and those that are less healthy become extinct. It is nature's way of keeping one step ahead of changes in an ecosystem.

INDUSTRIAL EXTREMOPHILES

The ultimate survivors are extremophiles. These are microbes related to the earliest forms of life on Earth. As their name suggests, they live in extreme conditions—very hot, very cold, very wet, very dry, acid, and alkali. They even live where you would not expect to find life at all.

Berkeley Pit near Butte, Montana, is an abandoned copper mine. It filled with rainwater, which became contaminated by chemicals, and is now acidic. In 1995, a flock of snow geese landed on the lake, drank the water, and some 340 birds died. Two local chemists, Don and Andrea Stierle, from Montana Tech of the University of Montana, decided to investigate lake sediments to find out if anything could live in such acid conditions. They found 42 living organisms (extremophiles) and some of the compounds they produce look to be promising as anti-cancer drugs.

The lake at Berkeley Pit is a defunct strip mine, where the water has turned distinctly acid from mining residues. Nevertheless, there are many organisms that thrive even here.

TIMELINE

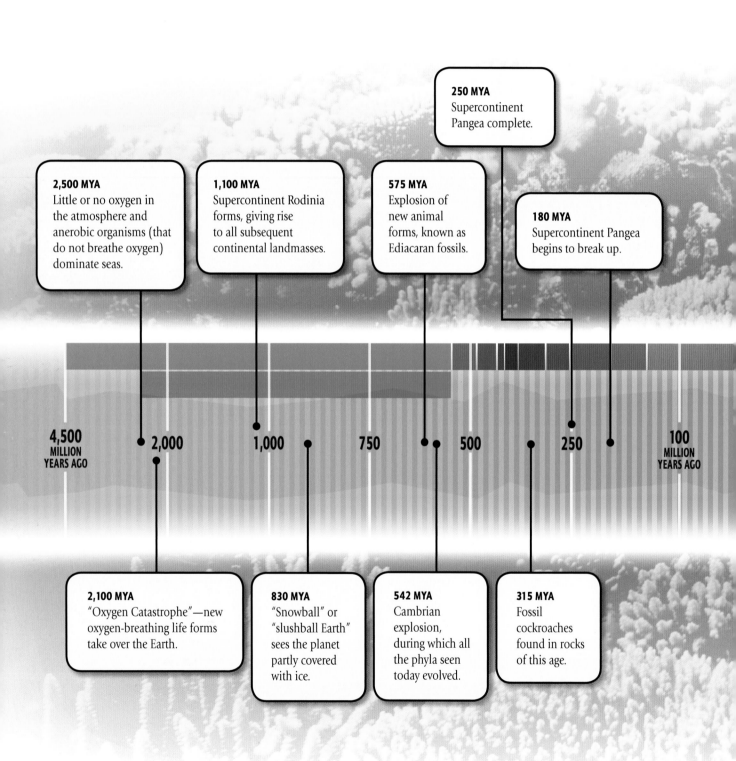

250 MYA
Supercontinent Pangea complete.

2,500 MYA
Little or no oxygen in the atmosphere and anerobic organisms (that do not breathe oxygen) dominate seas.

1,100 MYA
Supercontinent Rodinia forms, giving rise to all subsequent continental landmasses.

575 MYA
Explosion of new animal forms, known as Ediacaran fossils.

180 MYA
Supercontinent Pangea begins to break up.

4,500
MILLION
YEARS AGO

2,000

1,000

750

500

250

100
MILLION
YEARS AGO

2,100 MYA
"Oxygen Catastrophe"—new oxygen-breathing life forms take over the Earth.

830 MYA
"Snowball" or "slushball Earth" sees the planet partly covered with ice.

542 MYA
Cambrian explosion, during which all the phyla seen today evolved.

315 MYA
Fossil cockroaches found in rocks of this age.

MYA = Million years ago

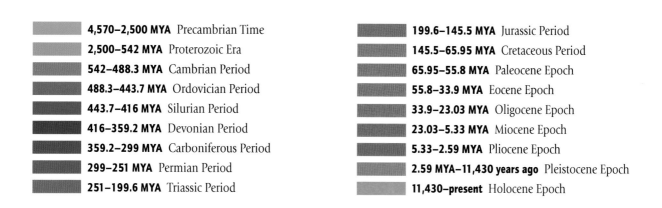

4,570–2,500 MYA Precambrian Time
2,500–542 MYA Proterozoic Era
542–488.3 MYA Cambrian Period
488.3–443.7 MYA Ordovician Period
443.7–416 MYA Silurian Period
416–359.2 MYA Devonian Period
359.2–299 MYA Carboniferous Period
299–251 MYA Permian Period
251–199.6 MYA Triassic Period

199.6–145.5 MYA Jurassic Period
145.5–65.95 MYA Cretaceous Period
65.95–55.8 MYA Paleocene Epoch
55.8–33.9 MYA Eocene Epoch
33.9–23.03 MYA Oligocene Epoch
23.03–5.33 MYA Miocene Epoch
5.33–2.59 MYA Pliocene Epoch
2.59 MYA–11,430 years ago Pleistocene Epoch
11,430–present Holocene Epoch

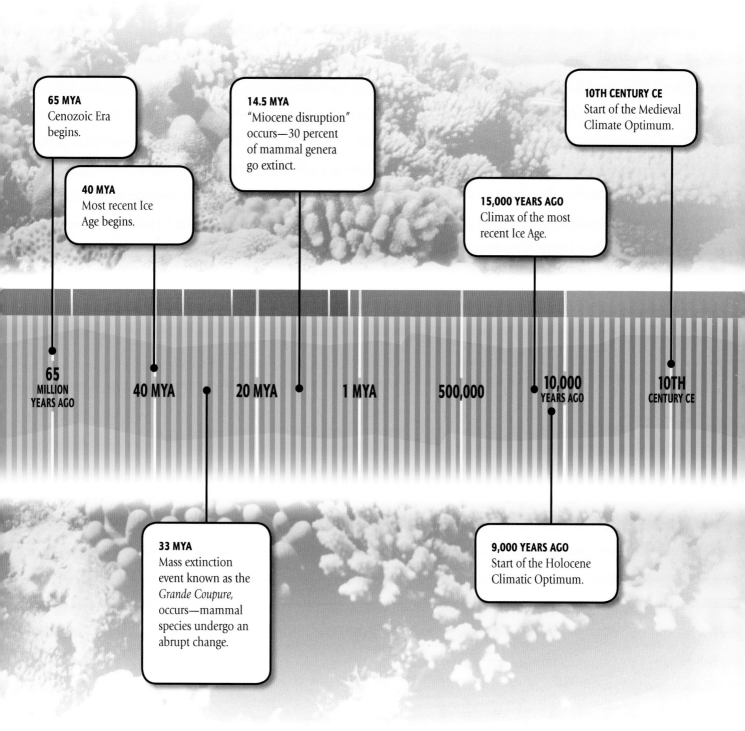

65 MYA
Cenozoic Era
begins.

40 MYA
Most recent Ice
Age begins.

14.5 MYA
"Miocene disruption"
occurs—30 percent
of mammal genera
go extinct.

10TH CENTURY CE
Start of the Medieval
Climate Optimum.

15,000 YEARS AGO
Climax of the most
recent Ice Age.

33 MYA
Mass extinction
event known as the
Grande Coupure,
occurs—mammal
species undergo an
abrupt change.

9,000 YEARS AGO
Start of the Holocene
Climatic Optimum.

65
MILLION
YEARS AGO

40 MYA

20 MYA

1 MYA

500,000

10,000
YEARS AGO

10TH
CENTURY CE

TIMELINE *CONTINUED*

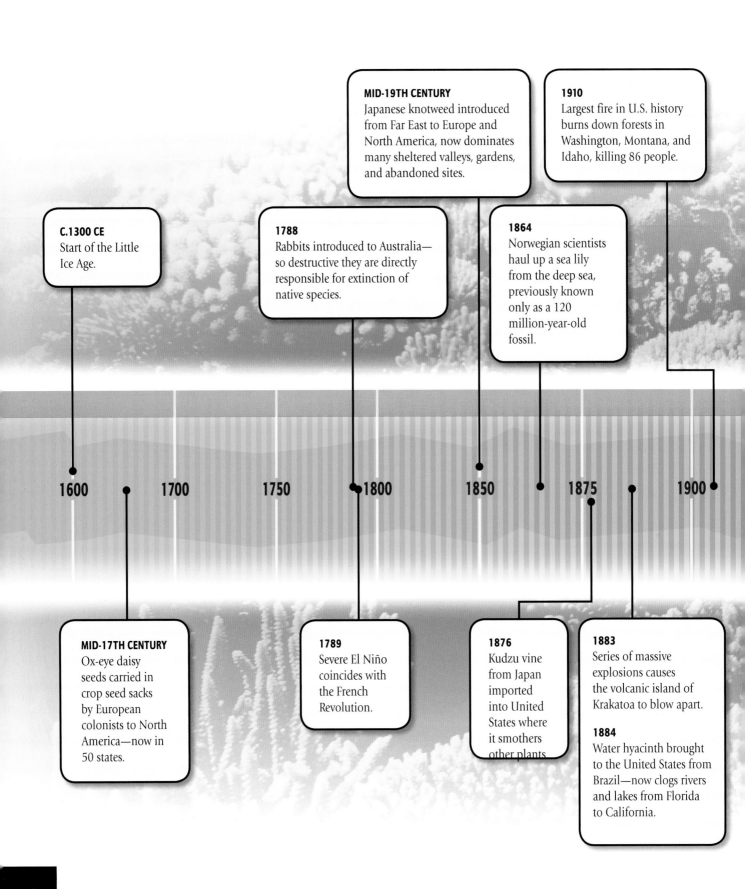

MID-19TH CENTURY
Japanese knotweed introduced from Far East to Europe and North America, now dominates many sheltered valleys, gardens, and abandoned sites.

1910
Largest fire in U.S. history burns down forests in Washington, Montana, and Idaho, killing 86 people.

C.1300 CE
Start of the Little Ice Age.

1788
Rabbits introduced to Australia—so destructive they are directly responsible for extinction of native species.

1864
Norwegian scientists haul up a sea lily from the deep sea, previously known only as a 120 million-year-old fossil.

1600   **1700**   **1750**   **1800**   **1850**   **1875**   **1900**

MID-17TH CENTURY
Ox-eye daisy seeds carried in crop seed sacks by European colonists to North America—now in 50 states.

1789
Severe El Niño coincides with the French Revolution.

1876
Kudzu vine from Japan imported into United States where it smothers other plants

1883
Series of massive explosions causes the volcanic island of Krakatoa to blow apart.

1884
Water hyacinth brought to the United States from Brazil—now clogs rivers and lakes from Florida to California.

4,570–2,500 MYA Precambrian Time	**199.6–145.5 MYA** Jurassic Period
2,500–542 MYA Proterozoic Era	**145.5–65.95 MYA** Cretaceous Period
542–488.3 MYA Cambrian Period	**65.95–55.8 MYA** Paleocene Epoch
488.3–443.7 MYA Ordovician Period	**55.8–33.9 MYA** Eocene Epoch
443.7–416 MYA Silurian Period	**33.9–23.03 MYA** Oligocene Epoch
416–359.2 MYA Devonian Period	**23.03–5.33 MYA** Miocene Epoch
359.2–299 MYA Carboniferous Period	**5.33–2.59 MYA** Pliocene Epoch
299–251 MYA Permian Period	**2.59 MYA–11,430 years ago** Pleistocene Epoch
251–199.6 MYA Triassic Period	**11,430–present** Holocene Epoch

1927
Anak Krakatoa, meaning "Child of Krakatoa," rises out of the sea.

C.1930
Dwight Billings' plant succession experiments conducted in United States.

1946
Paper bark trees, brought from Australia to United States, take over parts of the Everglades swamps like "living walls."

1979
Mineral chimneys known as black smokers discovered in the Gulf of California.

"Gaia hypothesis" book by James Lovelock published.

1982
Severe El Niño event coincides with extensive bush fires in Australia.

1984
Cold seep animal communities discovered on the floor of the Gulf of Mexico.

2003
Largest spate of wildfires in California's history, the "2003 Firestorm."

Canberra bush fires destroy 431 homes in Australia.

Canada's Okanagan Mountain Park loses 61,776 acres to fire.

United Kingdom rat population estimated as equal to human population.

1997
Ice worms discovered living on ice-like methane hydrate extrusions on the floor of the Gulf of Mexico.

1925   **1940**   **1965**   **1980**   **1995**   **2000**   **PRESENT DAY**

1935
Cane toad introduced to Australia as pest control—it is now a pest itself.

1936
Russian town of Kursha-2 in Siberia engulfed by wildfire, 1,200 people killed.

1977
Scientists discover deep-sea hydrothermal vent communities on the seabed near Galapagos Islands.

1980
Violent eruption of Mount St. Helens in North America.

1988
Worst fires in Yellowstone's history eventually put out by snow.

1990
Haakon Mosby mud volcano, with its own community of deep-sea animals, discovered on the floor of the Barents Sea.

1996
Polar scientists discover Lake Vostok, a vast underwater lake containing freshwater organisms, beneath the Antarctic ice sheet.

Fish-killing red algae identified in Chesapeake Bay on the east coast of the United States.

2004
6.5 million acres burned in Alaska's worst firestorm.

2007
Deadly fires in Greece kill 64 people.

900,000 people evacuated during Southern California wildfires.

FIND OUT MORE

Further reading

David, Laurie and Gordon, Cambria. *Down-to-Earth Guide to Global Warming*. New York: Scholastic, 2007.

Arnold, Caroline. *El Niño: Stormy Weather for People and Wildlife*. New York: Clarion Books, 2005.

Marrin , Albert. *Oh Rats! The Story of Rats and People.*. New York: Dutton Juvenile, 2006.

Winchester, Simon and Chin, Jason. *The Day the World Exploded: The Earthshaking Catastrophe at Krakatoa*. New York: HarperCollins, 2008.

Websites

The following websites will take you further into the subject of evolution and extinctions.

University of California Museum
of Paleontology
http://www.ucmp.berkeley.edu/index.php

University of California at Berkeley
http://evolution.berkeley.edu/evolibrary/
home.php

London's Natural History Museum
http://www.nhm.ac.uk

New York's American Museum of
Natural History
http://www.amnh.org

Smithsonian Institution
http://www.si.edu

Chicago's The Field Museum
http://www.fieldmuseum.org

Biology news

News of new developments in life sciences can be found at:
http://www.pbs.org/wgbh/nova/
sciencenow/involved/news.html
http://www.sciencedaily.com
http://sciencenow.sciencemag.org
http://www.newscientist.com/news.ns

To research

Find out more about El Niño and its impact both on South America and the rest of the world.

What happens to wildlife in different parts of the world during El Niño years? What is La Niña?

More information on El Niño, with up-to-date news, can be found at:
http://www.elnino.noaa.gov

Explore the 1980 eruption of Mount St. Helens in North America.

How did it differ from conventional eruptions? What was its impact on wildlife? Could anything survive such a blast and, if so, where would they have been hiding? How did ecosystems change and did they recover?

More information about Mount St. Helens can be found at:
http://www.fs.fed.us/gpnf/mshnvm
http://vulcan.wr.usgs.gov/Volcanoes/MSH

Volcano-cams of Mount St. Helens can be found at:
http://www.fs.fed.us/gpnf/volcanocams/msh

Examine the effects of abrupt changes, such as natural disasters, on wildlife communities.

What is the impact of earthquakes, landslides, snow and rock avalanches, tsunamis, droughts, floods, hurricanes, electrical storms, and tornados?

Find out more about extremophiles.

How could they be useful to humanity?

Useful sources of information on extremophiles are found at:
http://www.astrobiology.com/adastra/extremophiles.html
http://www.resa.net/nasa/otherextreme.htm

GLOSSARY

adaptation characteristic of an organism that enables it to be better suited to its environment

aerosol fine liquid droplets in a gas, which can come from volcanoes and aerosol spray cans

ammonite extinct group of marine mollusks, related to octopus, squid, and cuttlefish (cephalopods), which outwardly resemble the living pearly nautilus

anatomical related to the parts and systems of living bodies

annuals plant that germinates, flowers, and dies within one year, but reappears the following year

aquifer underground layer of water-bearing rock through which significant quantities of water flow

arson deliberately setting fire to something

atmosphere layer of gases surrounding Earth, kept in place by gravity

biome specific places on Earth where climate, vegetation, and landscape produce the same conditions and similar environments

biosphere part of Earth where life occurs

brine water saturated with salt

canopy habitat at the uppermost part of the forest

chemical cycling circuit or pathway by which a chemical moves through the biological (plants and animals) and non-biological (rocks, oceans, and atmosphere) components of an ecosystem. It can be an element, e.g. nitrogen, or a compound, e.g. water, and it is continuously recycled.

climax vegetation most mature and fully developed vegetation an ecosystem can achieve after a prolonged period of colonization

cold seep area of the ocean floor where hydrogen sulphide, methane, and other similar fluids ooze out from cracks in the rocks. It supports an unusual community of animals that don't rely on energy from the sun.

colonize when one or more species populates a new area

community group of organisms interacting in the same location

ecosystem specific area in which climate, landscape, and living organisms interact

energy flow flow of energy through a food chain or web

fossil fuel nonrenewable source of fuel formed from plants and animals that lived millions of years ago and found in the upper layers of Earth's crust. There are three major forms: coal, oil, and natural gas.

fronds leaf-like structures of algae (especially seaweeds) and ferns

gamma rays form of high-energy radiation or light emission with shorter wavelengths than X-rays. It kills living organisms and is produced when stars collide or explode.

genes units of inheritance that determine how an organism looks and the way it works

genus (plural: genera) unit of classification for a group of very similar species

germination process by which an organism comes out of a period when growth, development, and activity is temporarily suspended, e.g. the sprouting of a seedling

habitat place where an organism lives

hemisphere any half of the Earth, e.g. Northern Hemisphere, Southern Hemisphere, Western Hemisphere, Eastern Hemisphere

hibernation state of inactivity when an organism's body slows down to conserve energy

humidify to add water or moisture

hydrosphere all the water on Earth

hydrothermal vents cracks in the Earth's surface from which water, heated by energy from deep down in the Earth, flows

hypothesis tentative explanation for a phenomenon or event, while a theory is an explanation based on much data

light year unit, based on the speed of light, used to measure the enormous distances to the stars in the universe. One light year equals 5,878,625,373,183.61 miles (9,460,730,472,580.8 km).

lithosphere crust and upper mantle of Earth, i.e. the "solid" part

magma chamber highly-pressurized, large, underground reservoir of molten rock, beneath the Earth's surface, often with a volcano above

microbial mats layers of bacteria often growing in extreme conditions, e.g. hot springs or salt lakes

microclimate locality in which the climate differs from the surrounding area, e.g. a city street where the temperature is higher than the surrounding countryside

migration movement of organisms from one place to another

molten lava very hot liquid rock that flows from a volcano during an eruption—temperatures of 1,300-2,200°F (700-1,200°C)

oasis area of vegetation in a desert where there is a source of water

omnivore organism that eats both plant and animal food

ozone layer layer in the upper atmosphere (stratosphere) where most of Earth's ozone is found. It absorbs much of the sun's harmful ultraviolet radiation.

perennial plant that lives for more than two years. It dies back each winter but re-grows from the same rootstock the following spring.

photosynthesis process by which green plants, algae, and some bacteria use energy from sunlight to convert carbon dioxide and water into sugars and starch—the conversion of light energy into chemical energy

phylum (plural: phyla) term in the classification of living things that is below "kingdom" and above "class"

phytoplankton tiny drifting organisms that can manufacture their own food, e.g. algae

pioneer organisms that are first to establish in a new or dramatically modified habitat

plankton tiny drifting organisms that inhabit the sea, freshwater, or float in the air

plant succession various stages in the development of a plant community

poaching illegal hunting of wild animals

polyp sea anemone-like organisms

population collection of individuals of a particular species

precession change in the axis of a rotating object, such as Earth

primary consumer organism that gets its food and energy from a producer, e.g. herbivore

producer organisms that take energy from the sun or from the center of the Earth and use it to convert inorganic chemicals into food, e.g. green plants and cyanobacteria

rads what radiation is measured in

relict animal or plant that has survived while others in its group are extinct

scrub plant community dominated by scattered low-growing plants, including shrubs, grasses, and herbs

secondary consumer organism that gets its food and energy from other consumers, e.g. a carnivore

selection pressure aspect of the environment (such as climate, competitors, and potential partners) that stresses an organism, giving it either an advantage over other organisms or eliminating it completely

soil litter layer of dead leaves and other plant debris on the forest floor

symbiotic relationship relationship between two organisms in which at least one benefits

temperate in geography, this refers to the lands between the tropics and Polar Regions

terrestrial living on land

tinder dry material that can easily catch fire

tundra area where tree growth is limited by cold temperatures and a short growing season. There are two types—Arctic tundra in the Arctic, and Antarctic and alpine tundra above the treeline in mountains.

ultraviolet radiation light at the blue end of the light spectrum that is invisible to humans. It is a harmful part of the sun's rays because it causes sunburn and skin cancer.

understory layer of plants in a forest between the ground and canopy

vascular related to blood vessels or the transportation system of higher plants

vertebrate animal with a backbone

INDEX